Windows Xp Sp3 Install Guide

by

Cyber Jannah Studio

2018

Preface

Windows XP (codenamed Whistler) is a personal computer operating system that was produced by Microsoft as part of the Windows NT family of operating systems. It was released to manufacturing on August 24, 2001, and broadly released for retail sale on October 25, 2001.

Development of Windows XP began in the late 1990s as "Neptune", an operating system built on the Windows NT kernel which was intended specifically for mainstream consumer use. An updated version of Windows 2000 was also originally planned for the business market; however, in January 2000, both projects were shelved in favor of a single OS codenamed "Whistler", which would serve as a single OS platform for both consumer and business markets. As such, Windows XP was the first consumer edition of Windows not to be based on MS-DOS.

Upon its release, Windows XP received generally positive reviews, with critics noting increased performance and stability (especially in comparison to Windows ME), a more intuitive user interface, improved hardware support, and expanded multimedia capabilities. However, some industry reviewers were concerned by the new licensing model and product activation system.

Extended support for Windows XP ended on April 8, 2014, after which the operating system ceased receiving further support or security updates to most users. As of May 2018, 2.98% of Windows PCs run Windows XP, and therefore XP represents 2.5% of the overall desktop operating system market share. In the late 1990s, initial development of what would become Windows XP was focused on two individual products; "Odyssey", which was reportedly intended to succeed the future Windows 2000, and "Neptune", which was reportedly a consumer-oriented operating system using the Windows NT architecture, succeeding the MS-DOS-based Windows 98.

However, the projects proved to be too ambitious. In January 2000, shortly prior to the official release of Windows 2000, technology writer Paul Thurrott reported that Microsoft had shelved both Neptune and Odyssey in favor of a new product codenamed "Whistler", after Whistler, British Columbia, as many Microsoft employees skied at the Whistler-Blackcomb ski resort.[9] The goal of Whistler was to unify both the consumer and business-oriented Windows lines under a single, Windows NT platform: Thurrott stated that Neptune had become "a black hole when all the features that were cut from [Windows ME] were simply re-tagged as Neptune features. And since Neptune and Odyssey would be based on the same code-base anyway, it made sense to combine them into a single project".

At PDC on July 13, 2000, Microsoft announced that Whistler would be released during the second half of 2001, and also unveiled the first preview build, 2250. The build notably introduced an early version of Windows XP's visual styles system.

In June 2001, Microsoft indicated that it was planning to, in conjunction with Intel and other PC makers, spend at least 1 billion US dollars on marketing and promoting Windows XP. The theme of the campaign, "Yes You Can", was designed to emphasize the platform's overall capabilities.

Microsoft had originally planned to use the slogan "Prepare to Fly", but it was replaced due to sensitivity issues in the wake of the September 11 attacks.

On August 24, 2001, Windows XP build 2600 was released to manufacturing. During a ceremonial media event at Microsoft Redmond Campus, copies of the RTM build were given to representatives of several major PC manufacturers in briefcases, who then flew off on decorated helicopters. While PC manufacturers would be able to release devices running XP beginning on September 24, 2001, XP was expected to reach general retail availability on October 25, 2001. On the same day, Microsoft also announced the final retail pricing of XP's two main editions, "Home" and "Professional".

Microsoft released the first beta build of Whistler, build 2296, on October 31, 2000. Subsequent builds gradually introduced features that users of the release version of Windows XP would recognise, such as Internet Explorer 6.0, the Microsoft Product Activation system and the Bliss desktop background.

On February 5, 2001, Microsoft officially announced that Whistler would be known as Windows XP, where XP stands for "eXPerience".

In June 2001, Microsoft indicated that it was planning to, in conjunction with Intel and other PC makers, spend at least 1 billion US dollars on marketing and promoting Windows XP. The theme of the campaign, "Yes You Can", was designed to emphasize the platform's overall capabilities. Microsoft had originally planned to use the slogan "Prepare to Fly", but it was replaced due to sensitivity issues in the wake of the September 11 attacks.

On August 24, 2001, Windows XP build 2600 was released to manufacturing. During a ceremonial media event at Microsoft Redmond Campus, copies of the RTM build were given to representatives of several major PC manufacturers in briefcases, who then flew off on decorated helicopters. While PC manufacturers would be able to release devices running XP beginning on September 24, 2001, XP was expected to reach general retail availability on October 25, 2001. On the same day, Microsoft also announced the final retail pricing of XP's two main editions, "Home" and "Professional".

Tutorial How To Install Windows Xp Sp3

1) Shall we begin? (Image 1.1)

After configuring the system for booting from a CD or Live USB, the Windows Setup screen appears. To create Windows Xp Sp3 Live USB from ISO we can use free tool WinSetupFromUSB or Yumi Pendrive Linux.

At this point, Setup is loading the driver files it needs to continue with installation.

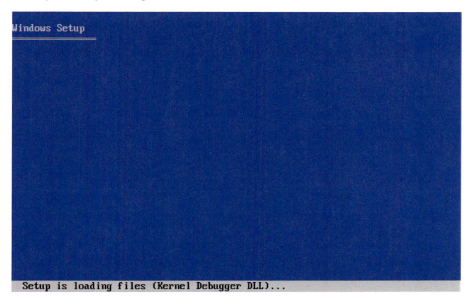

1) Shall we begin? (Image 1.1)

2) Welcome to Setup: (Image 1.2)

The "Welcome to Setup" screen appears with the option of Continuing Setup, Repair a previous installation, or Quitting.

Press ENTER to Continue Setup.

You may also choose R to Repair, or F3 to Quit and reboot the system.

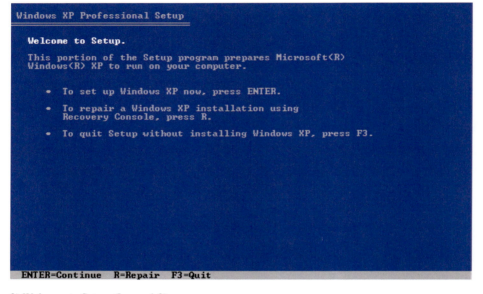

2) Welcome to Setup: (Image 1.2)

3) Windows XP Licensing Agreement: (Image 1.3)

The "Windows XP Licensing Agreement" screen, otherwise known as "EULA," displays the legal in's and out's of this particular software package.

You may press F8 to signify that you agree with the terms, hit ESC if you do not agree and PAGE UP or PAGE DOWN to scroll through each screen. Note: If you do not agree to the terms, setup will quit and reboot the system.

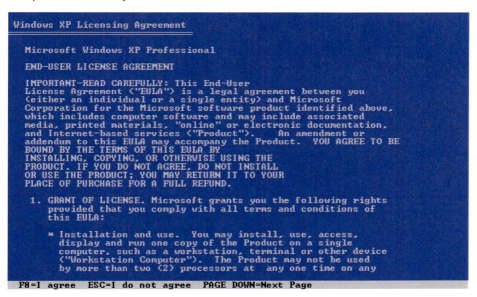

3) Windows XP Licensing Agreement: (Image 1.3)

4) Hard drive partition information: (Image 1.4)

Hard drive partition information is now displayed. This varies with each systems hardware configuration.

This example already has a partition defined. I will choose not to use this and create a new one by pressing D.
You may skip this and the next few steps if you do not have any partitions defined.

At this point, the options include pressing ENTER to Install on the selected partition, D to Delete the selected partition, or F3 to Quit and reboot the system.

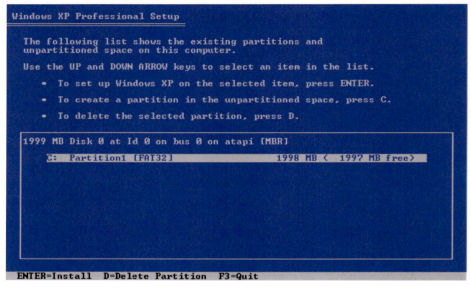

4) Hard drive partition information: (Image 1.4)

5) Warning screen: (Image 1.5)

After pressing D to delete the selected partition, a warning screen appears explaining the pitfalls of deleting it. This particular screen only appears when the partition selected to be deleted is formatted as a bootable system partition. Other partitions will display the next screen.

I want this to happen, so I press ENTER to continue.

The options include pressing ENTER to continue, or ESC to Cancel.

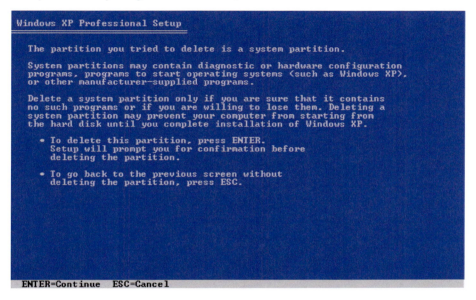

5) Warning screen: (Image 1.5)

6) Confirmation screen: (Image 1.6)

A confirmation screen that displays the logical drive, what file system the partition is currently using, the size in MB and controller information.

Options include L to Delete the partition and ESC to Cancel the action.

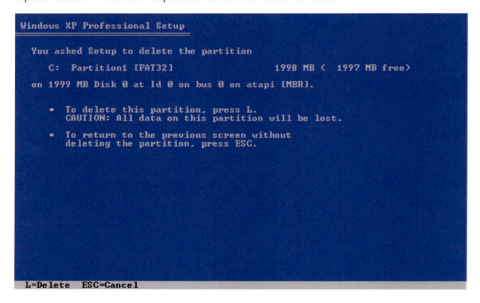

6) Confirmation screen: (Image 1.6)

7) No partitions have been previously defined: (Image 1.7)

If no partitions have been previously defined, this screen will be displayed. You may section your hard drive in as many partitions as you wish by selecting C to Create a Partition and then entering in a value less then the total available. Here, I will Create a Partition in the highlighted, unused portion.

Select the partition you wish to install to using the UP arrow and DOWN ARROW keys.

Press ENTER to use the highlighted partition and Install, C to Create a Partition, or F3 to Quit and reboot the system.

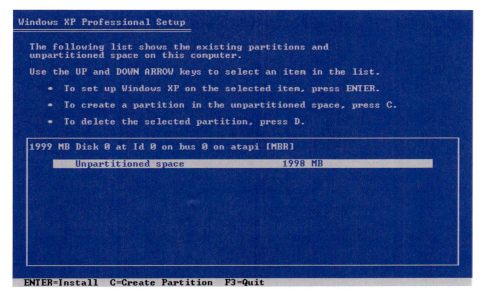

7) No partitions have been previously defined: (Image 1.7)

8) Enter in the partition size: (Image 1.8)

Enter in the partition size in MB within the displayed minimum and maximum. I chose the default or maximum available here.

You may choose ENTER to Create the new partition or ESC to Cancel the action.

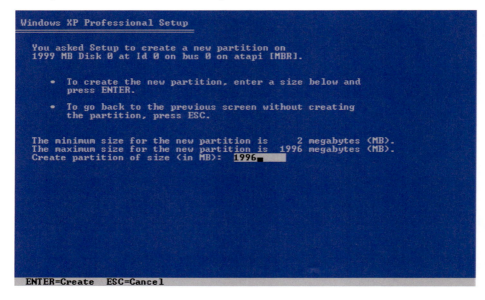

8) Enter in the partition size: (Image 1.8)

9) Continue to create partitions : (Image 1.9)

Continue to create partitions until all space is used or the configuration meets your requirements. Note: a small portion will be unavailable to partition. This is normal. In this example, it is 2 MB.

I chose drive C: or Partition1 to install the Operating System.

You may choose ENTER to Install to the selected partition, D to Delete the highlighted Partition, or F3 to Quit and reboot the system.

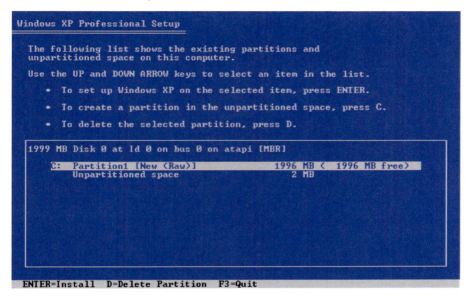

9) Continue to create partitions: (Image 1.9)

10) Format the partition: (Image 1.10)

Since this OS supports NTFS, format the partition with it. If you do not, many folder and file security features will be unavailable. Note: If you are dual booting your system, a previous OS will not be able to read the local information. This is a fact with Windows 9x and Me. If you have a requirement to view this partition from another OS installed on the system, do not format it as NTFS. Also, the boot partition must be formatted with FAT32 if you wish to dual boot. I have found no problems accessing a NTFS partition mapped as a network drive from an older OS.

Select what format you wish to use by pressing the UP ARROW and DOWN ARROW keys.

Press ENTER to confirm your selection and Continue or ESC to Cancel.

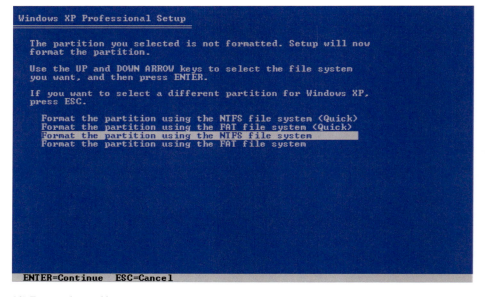

10) Format the partition: (Image 1.10)

11) Setup formats the partition: (Image 1.11)

Watch the progress bar as Setup formats the partition. or get up and get a soda. It may take awhile.

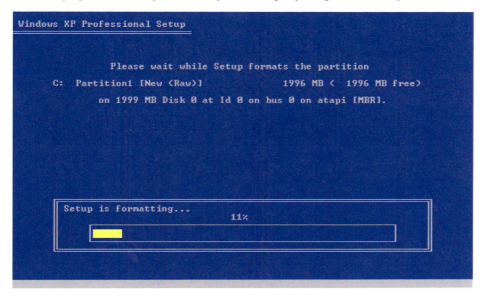

11) Setup formats the partition: (Image 1.11)

12) Creating File List: (Image 1.12)

Setup is now figuring out what files to copy over to the hard drive.

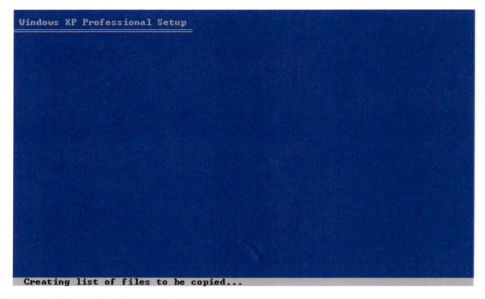

12) Creating File List: (Image 1.12)

13) Setup copies various files: (Image 1.13)

After the partition is finished formatting, Setup copies various files to support booting from the hard drive and continue on.

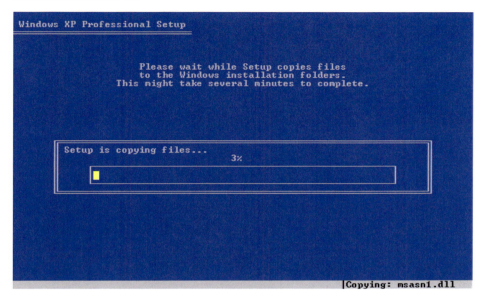

13) Setup copies various files: (Image 1.13)

14) Creates various information files: (Image 1.14)

Setup then creates various information files required to continue on with setup.

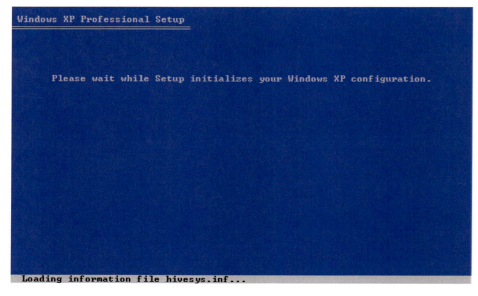

14) Creates various information files: (Image 1.14)

15) Press ENTER to Restart: (Image 1.15)

The first reboot and the end of the blue background has arrived. If you are impatient, press ENTER to Restart before the 15 seconds expire.

ENTER to Restart the Computer is the only option available.

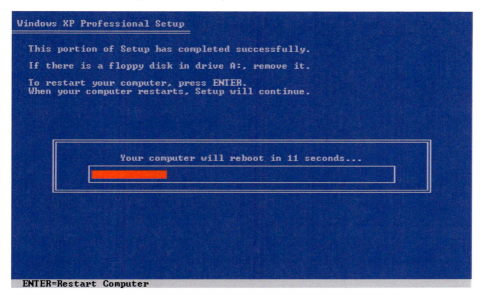

15) Press ENTER to Restart: (Image 1.15)

16) Windows XP boot screen: (Image 2.1)

The new Windows XP boot screen is displayed.

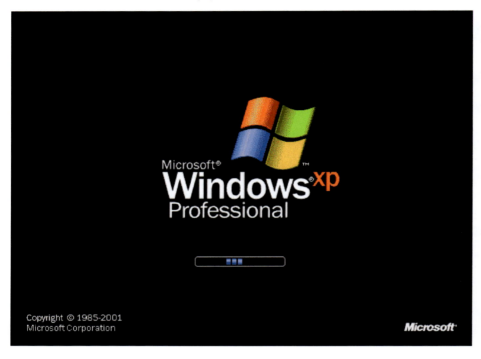

16) Windows XP boot screen: (Image 2.1)

17) Windows XP Installation: (Image 2.2)

If you have installed Windows before, this type of screen will look familiar.

Sit back. It may be awhile.

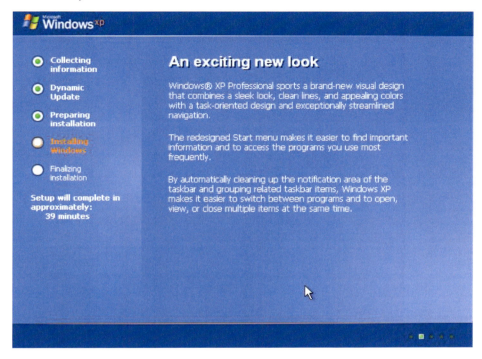

17) Windows XP Installation: (Image 2.2)

18) Faster and more reliable: (Image 2.3)

Every Windows OS that comes out has the same claim. Faster and better. It is subject to debate whether or not it could get "any worse."

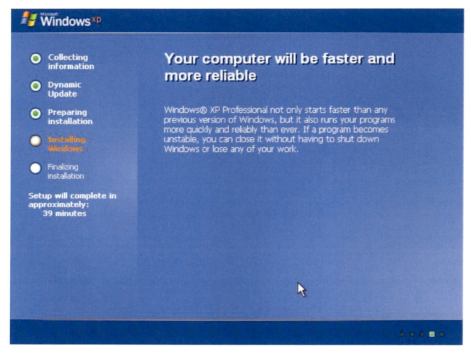

18) Faster and more reliable: (Image 2.3)

19) Region and Input Languages: (Image 2.4)

A little while later, you will be prompted with options of configuring your Region and Input Languages. The default was fine for me, so I selected Next.

Options include **Customize** button, **Details** Button, plus the standard **Back** and **Next**.

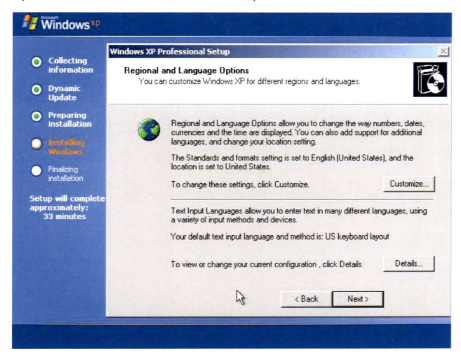

19) Region and Input Languages: (Image 2.4)

20) Enter in your Name: (Image 2.5)

Enter in your Name and optional Organization information, then select the **Next** button.

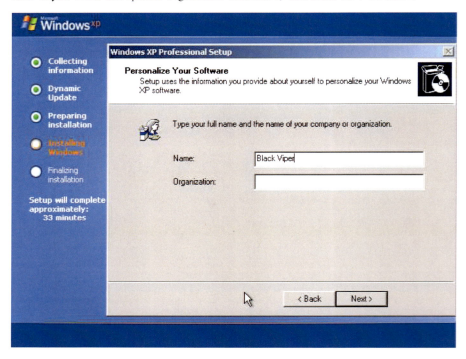

20) Enter in your Name: (Image 2.5)

21) 25 digit Product Key: (Image 2.6)

Thought you could get away from it? Think again.

Enter your unique 25 digit Product Key that came with your CD, then select the **Next** button.

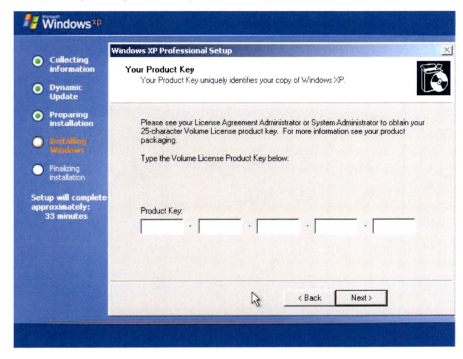

21) 25 digit Product Key: (Image 2.6)

22) Enter a Computer name and an Administrator Password: (Image 2.7)

The "suggested" name for the computer is always really whacked out. Choose one that meets your needs.

Enter an Administrator Password now. It is VERY IMPORTANT that you keep this information safe and remember what it is! "01Pa$$word" is not a good choice. Think of something secure and never lose or forget it.

22) Enter a Computer name and an Administrator Password: (Image 2.7)

23) Date, Time and Time Zone: (Image 2.8)

Configure the proper information for the Date, Time and Time Zone here.

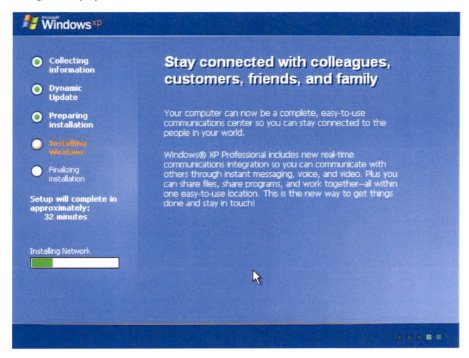

24) Network is installing: (Image 2.9)

24) Network is installing: (Image 2.9)

Wait here while the Network is installing. You could read all the marketing dribble, but I do not recommend it. ☺

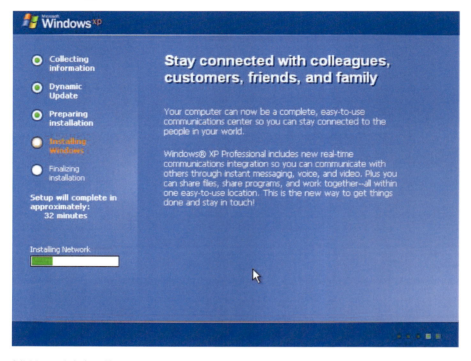

24) Network is installing: (Image 2.9)

25) Network Settings Dialog: (Image 3.1)

The Network Settings Dialog is next. Under usual circumstances, the **Typical settings** are fine, but I never choose them so I can poke around under the hood. I selected **Custom settings** here.

Choose your method and select the **Next** button.

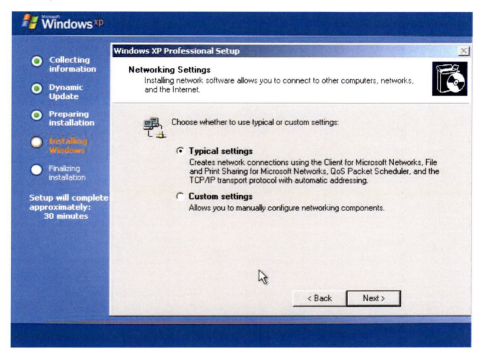

25) Network Settings Dialog: (Image 3.1)

26) Custom settings: (Image 3.2)

In the **Custom settings**, many options are abound. I cannot go into all of them here, but I will hit on the high points.

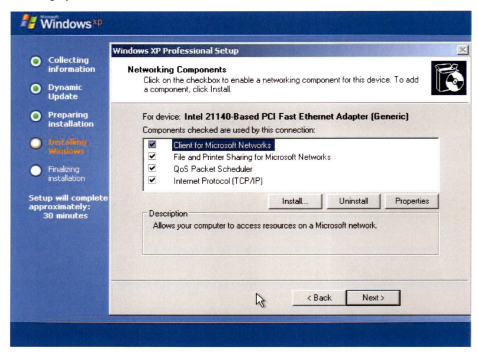

26) Custom settings: (Image 3.2)

27) QoS Packet Scheduler: (Image 3.3)

QoS Packet Scheduler is not required unless your network uses it.

For this system, I will choose to **uncheck** it.

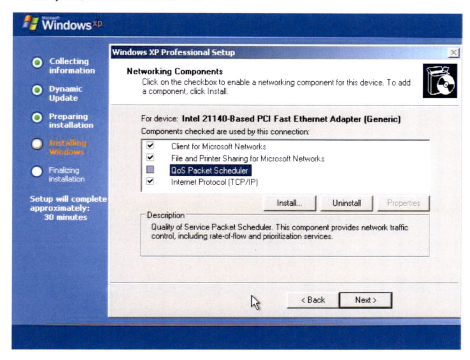

27) QoS Packet Scheduler: (Image 3.3)

28) TCP/IP Properties: (Image 3.4)

TCP/IP Properties contains the standard options. Adjust them for your particular needs as required. For now, I kept the default settings. Basically, it is using DHCP to configure TCP/IP. If you are using a static IP address, enter in the proper information here.

Select the **Advanced** button to further configure your TCP/IP options.

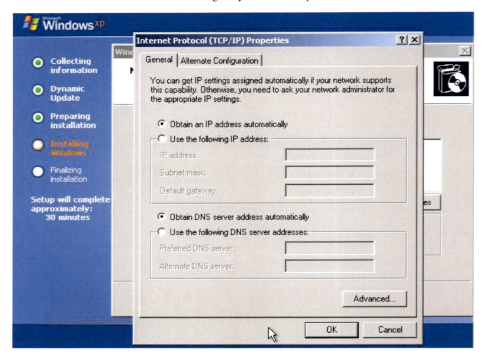

28) TCP/IP Properties: (Image 3.4)

29) Workgroup or Computer Domain: (Image 3.5)

Workgroup or Computer Domain, that is the question. I am not going to set up this system to connect to a domain controller, so I will place it as a member of a workgroup.

Please, change "WORKGROUP" to something else. I hate defaults. ☺

Select the Next button after making your choice.

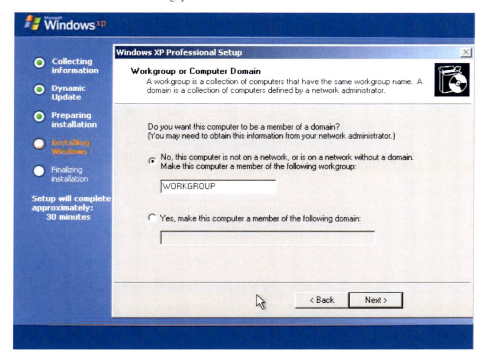

29) Workgroup or Computer Domain: (Image 3.5)

30) Install screen: (Image 3.6)

The system will reboot after all files have been copied over to the install partition. Now may be a good time to take a break. It may be awhile.

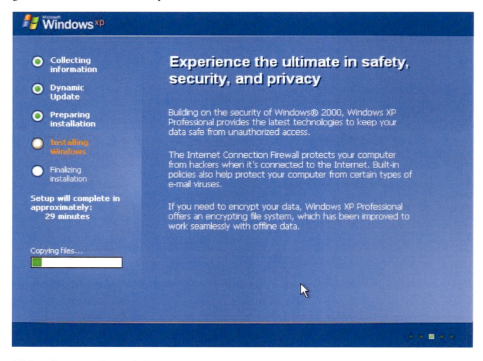

30) Install screen: (Image 3.6)

31) Windows XP is starting up: (Image 4.1)

The moment we have all been waiting for, Windows XP Professional is starting up "for the first time." Remember that quoted statement with Windows 95 setup?

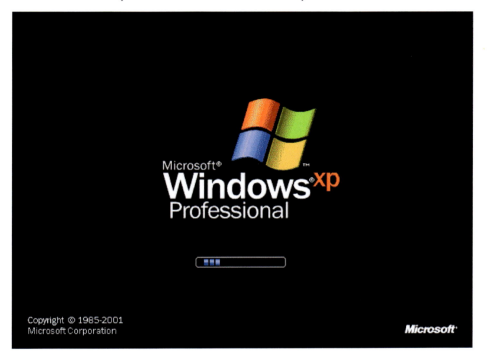

31) Windows XP is starting up: (Image 4.1)

32) Display Settings Pop-up: (Image 4.2)

Windows XP no longer likes the "default" resolution of 640 x 480 and prompts you of that fact.

Select **OK** to continue.

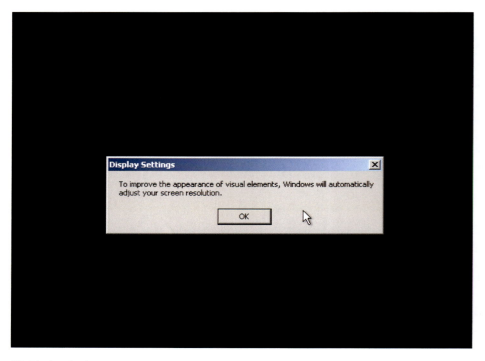

32) Display Settings Pop-up: (Image 4.2)

33) Please wait: (Image 4.3)

800 x 600 is a wonderful thing, however, I chose to have it time out and return to 640 x 480 for this guide.

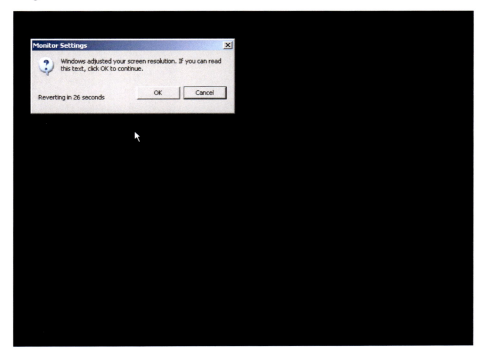

33) Please wait: (Image 4.3)

34) Login to the Administrator account: (Image 4.4)

With the "Welcome" screen, you no longer have to hit the "Three Finger Salute" combination of Ctrl+Alt+Delete to login to the Administrator account.

You did remember your password, right?!?

34) Login to the Administrator account: (Image 4.4)

35) Applying computer settings: (Image 4.5)

Please wait while the Administrator account is configured "for the first time."

No. I will not mention Windows 95 again...

35) Applying computer settings: (Image 4.5)

36) Display Settings Pop-up: (Image 4.6)

Since the initial screen resolution is set to 640 x 480, a balloon dialog appears. You may click the pop-up balloon to raise the resolution up to 800 x 600 automatically. For the rest of this guide, I chose to ignore it.

36) Display Settings Pop-up: (Image 4.6)

37) Windows XP tour: (Image 5.1)

Click the balloon dialog to start a tour of Windows XP.

Even if you do not wish to see the information, you should click on the balloon to get rid of the annoyance in a timely fashion.

37) Windows XP tour: (Image 5.1)

38) Windows XP Tour dialog: (Image 5.2)

Windows XP Tour dialog popup is shown.

Select the **Cancel** button to never see it again.

38) Windows XP Tour dialog: (Image 5.2)

39) .NET Passport Wizard: (Image 5.3)

Double-Click   the   Messenger   Icon   in   the   bottom   right   (system   tray)   and   the   ".NET
Passport Wizard" dialog appears.

Select **Cancel** to not sign up for Passport at this time.

39) .NET Passport Wizard: (Image 5.3)

40) Windows Messenger: (Image 5.4)

With the .NET Passport Wizard gone, the Windows Messenger is opened.

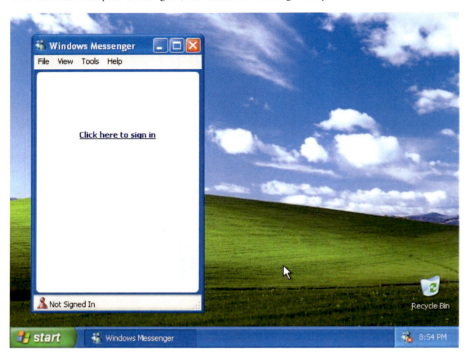

40) Windows Messenger: (Image 5.4)

41) Windows Messenger Tools: (Image 5.5)

Select **Tools**, then **Options**.

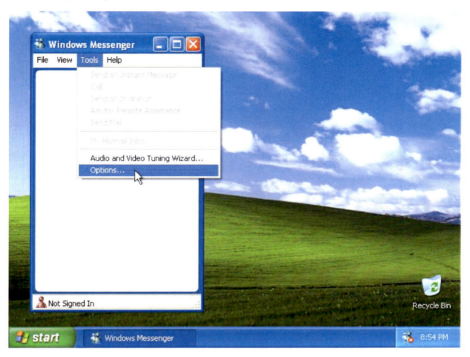

41) Windows Messenger Tools: (Image 5.5)

42) Messenger Preferences: (Image 5.6)

In the Options window, select the Preferences Tab.

Uncheck "Run this program when Windows starts" and "Allow this program to run in the background." Of course, if you wish to keep Windows Messenger, do not do this step.

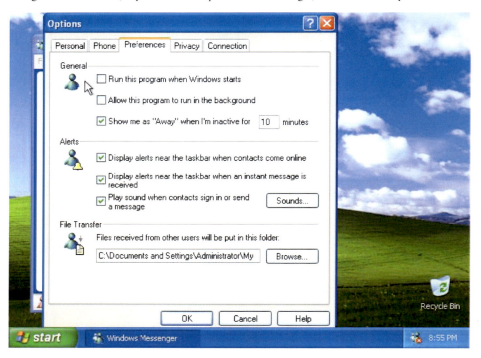

42) Messenger Preferences: (Image 5.6)

43) Close Messenger: (Image 5.7)

Now you can select the **Close** button and Messenger will be unloaded from memory.

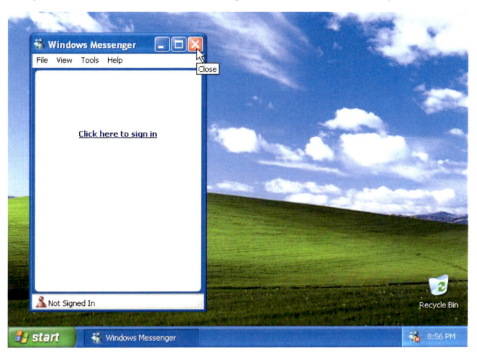

43) Close Messenger: (Image 5.7)

Epilog

That's all there is to it! I hope this guide helped you out or gave you a sneak peek at what is to come. Windows Xp Sp3 is old and ancient but still good for education and research.

.